LOVE PERSONIFIED
The Climax of the Gospel

FOUR STORIES TOLD IN ONE
As Recorded in the New American Standard Bible

Enid F. Hands

TEACH Services, Inc.
P U B L I S H I N G
www.TEACHServices.com • (800) 367-1844

World rights reserved. This book or any portion thereof may not be copied or reproduced in any form or manner whatever, except as provided by law, without the written permission of the publisher, except by a reviewer who may quote brief passages in a review.

The author assumes full responsibility for the accuracy of all facts and quotations as cited in this book. The opinions expressed in this book are the author's personal views and interpretations and do not necessarily reflect those of the publisher.

This book is provided with the understanding that the publisher is not engaged in giving spiritual, legal, medical, or other professional advice. If authoritative advice is needed, the reader should seek the counsel of a competent professional.

Copyright © 2024 Enid F. Hands
Copyright © 2024 TEACH Services, Inc.
ISBN-13: 978-1-4796-1731-9 (Paperback)
ISBN-13: 978-1-4796-1732-6 (ePub)
Library of Congress Control Number: 2024905716

Original material copyright © 2023 by Enid F. Hands

Scripture quotations, unless otherwise indicated, are taken from the (NASB®) New American Standard Bible®, Copyright © 1960, 1971, 1977, 1995, 2020 by The Lockman Foundation. Used by permission. All rights reserved. www.lockman.org.

Scripture quotations marked KJV are taken from King James Version. Public domain.

Editor: Lester Hands
Artwork: Anna Krouze
Back cover photograph: Gregory Schneider

Published by

www.TEACHServices.com • (800) 367-1844

For my son, Lester, who was so helpful in preparing this work.

CONTENTS

Foreword	viii
Preface	ix
Acknowledgments	x
Prologue	xi
THURSDAY	**13**
Preparation for the Passover	13
Jesus Remakes the Passover Supper	13
The Disciples Argue about Greatness	14
Jesus Demonstrates Greatness	14
Jesus Identifies His Betrayer	15
Jesus Predicts Peter's Denial	16
Jesus in Agony	16
Jesus Is Betrayed and Arrested	17
Devotional Thoughts for Thursday	18
FRIDAY	**19**
Jesus before the High Priest	19
Jesus before the Sanhedrin	20
Peter Denies Jesus and Weeps	20
Jesus before Pilate	21

Judas Hangs Himself	22
Jesus before Herod	22
Jesus or Barabbas	23
Jesus Crucified	24
Jesus Dies on the Cross	26
Jesus' Side Is Pierced	27
Jesus Buried in Joseph's Tomb	27
Devotional Thoughts for Friday	28

SABBATH — 30

A Guard Is Set	30
Devotional Thoughts for Sabbath	30

SUNDAY — 32

He Is Risen	32
Mary Magdalene Sees Jesus	33
The Soldiers Are Bribed	33
The Road to Emmaus	34
Jesus Appears before His Disciples	35
Devotional Thoughts for Sunday	35

THE FORTY DAYS — 37

Jesus Commissions His Disciples	37
Seeing and Believing	38
Breakfast by the Sea	38
Peter Is Restored	39
The Beloved Disciple	40
Jesus Ascends to Heaven	40
Concluding Devotional Thoughts	40

POSTSCRIPT	**43**
Reason to Believe	43
Appendix	**44**
Resources	**53**
Bibliography	**54**

FOREWORD

Enid Hands has taken the gospel narrative from the three synoptic authors, and united them with the beloved apostle John's Gospel perspective. She has achieved a flow of thought and inspiration that brings the privileged reader into the very presence of the world's Redeemer, as He offered Himself a sacrifice and paid the penalty for the sins of His own creation: the citizens of this world. Combining the climactic final week of Jesus' ministry into one beautiful stream, presenting Christ's compassion, care, and immeasurable love for the human race, brings added depth and continuity to the account and almost magnetically draws the human heart to the very source of love and life and truth: Jesus Christ!

Let me mention two vital aspects that Enid Hands has been inspired to include. One truly beautiful feature that is included for each day, Thursday through Sunday, of the final week of the gospel narrative, is a Devotional Thought from the great classic on the life of Christ, *Desire of Ages,* by Ellen White. These insights into the remarkable events as they unfolded in the divine plan of salvation, inspire and further draw the heart of the reader to the One who has given us life and offers us life eternal! Another key feature is the appendix. It is so easy when reading a choice book, to completely ignore the appendix. You won't want to do that here! You'll find important historical information and context that can provide valuable clarity.

As you contemplate these inspired words of the good news of salvation, may each reader be immensely blessed, and God be praised and glorified by this precious and remarkable revelation of the gospel of Jesus Christ!

Ted Phelps
Silverton, Oregon

PREFACE

I began this work at the time when COVID 19 confined us to our homes. I wanted to condense the closing scenes of Christ's sacrifice for each of us into a flowing narrative that would include the important parts of each Gospel. With the passage of time, the work was laid aside. When I recently reread the four Gospels, I felt the nudge to pick up the unfinished work and complete it.

What is to be gained by reading the combined story of the four Gospels? One benefit is that all the important and interesting details come together in one presentation. For example, the stories about the angel that came to strengthen Jesus, and the thief on the cross, are found only in Luke; and the story of Jesus committing His mother to His disciple John before He died is mentioned only by John.

> *To gain the whole picture of the climax of the gospel story, one has to experience the details that are included in all four Gospels—ideally taking time to slowly ponder each day separately.*

Is not each Gospel sufficient in itself? The Gospels were written under the guidance of the Holy Spirit (2 Peter 1:21) for different purposes and by individuals with very different personalities.

We could liken the Gospels to the well-known story of the elephant and the four blind men. When each blind man touched a different part of the elephant, and was asked to describe what he felt, the response of each was different. So also with the Gospel writers; each had, as it were, his own fingerprint on it. To gain the whole picture of the climax of the gospel story, one has to experience the details that are included in all four Gospels—ideally taking time to slowly ponder each day separately.

Finally and very importantly, I wish to acknowledge that I have strongly felt the promptings and guidance of the Holy Spirit as this work has progressed.

ACKNOWLEDGMENTS

My first acknowledgment and thanks goes to my son, Lester, for the major contribution he has made in so many areas of making this work printable. His expertise on the computer and advice have been invaluable. This work would not be here without his tireless efforts. Credit must also be given to him for the prologue and appendix.

Secondly, I am very grateful for the artwork at the beginning of each new day. Anna Krouze's artwork brings more clearly to the imagination the scenes portrayed in the text. She is to be commended too for her gracious and willing spirit which was so evident as I worked with her.

Credit for the back cover photo goes to my grandson, Gregory Schneider. Finally, I am grateful for the editing help which my husband, Arthur, and daughter, Irma, have given.

PROLOGUE

The place is ancient Israel, then called Judea and Galilee. The time is 2,000 years ago. The Roman Empire extended from western Europe to the Middle East.

Because of their unique religion and national identity, subjugation of the Jews had been a challenge for Rome and a source of constant irritation for the Jews. No other people had a religion that proclaimed a single God above all other gods. No other people refused to bow the knee to the emperor. No other people believed that soon a Messiah would arise and deliver them from the bondage of Rome.

Into this volatile part of the Roman Empire came a teacher from the small village of Nazareth in the hill country of Galilee. Proclaiming Himself to be the "Son of God," yet He lived a humble itinerant life, associating with commoners, tax collectors (despised because they were seen as cooperating with the hated Romans), and prostitutes. He quickly became very popular but alienated the Jewish ruling class, who became determined to eliminate Him no matter the cost.

We start our story when Jesus of Nazareth was about thirty-three years old at the time of the Jewish Passover. This festival was a memorial of an event when the Jews had been liberated from slavery some 2,000 years before. Many believed that Jesus would at this time proclaim Himself to be the Messiah and summon the armies of heaven to throw off the Roman yoke. They had seen Him heal the sick, feed a multitude with just five loaves of bread and two fishes, and even raise the dead back to life.

Jesus invites just twelve of those who followed Him (disciples) to share the Passover supper with him. What happens at that supper and in the following few days completely shatters their expectations and gives birth to a new way of life that will in a few centuries engulf the Roman Empire.

THURSDAY

Preparation for the Passover

Mark 14:12–16

On the first day of Unleavened Bread, when the Passover lamb was being sacrificed, His disciples said to Him, "Where do You want us to go and prepare for You to eat the Passover?"

And He sent two of His disciples and said to them, "Go into the city, and a man carrying a pitcher of water will meet you; follow him; and wherever he enters, say to the owner of the house, 'The Teacher says, "Where is My guest room in which I may eat the Passover with My disciples?"' And he himself will show you a large upstairs room furnished and ready; prepare for us there." The disciples left and came to the city and found everything just as He had told them; and they prepared the Passover.

Jesus Remakes the Passover Supper

Luke 22:14–23

When the hour came, He reclined at the table, and the apostles with Him. And He said to them, "I have eagerly desired to eat this Passover with you before I suffer; for I say to you, I shall not eat it again until it is fulfilled in the kingdom of God."

And when He had taken a cup and given thanks, He said, "Take this and share it among yourselves; for I say to you, I will not drink of the fruit of the vine from now on until the kingdom of God comes."

And when He had taken some bread and given thanks, He broke it and gave it to them, saying, "This is My body, which is being given for you; do this in remembrance of Me."

And in the same way He took the cup after they had eaten, saying, "This cup, which is poured out for you, is the new covenant in My blood. But behold, the hand of the one betraying Me is with Mine on the table. For indeed, the Son of Man is going as it has been determined; but woe to that man by whom He is betrayed!"

And they began to debate among themselves which one of them it was who was going to do this.

The Disciples Argue about Greatness

Luke 22:24-30

And a dispute also developed among them as to which one of them was regarded as being the greatest. And He said to them, "The kings of the Gentiles domineer over them; and those who have authority over them are called 'Benefactors.' But it is not this way for you; rather, the one who is the greatest among you must become like the youngest, and the leader like the servant. For who is greater, the one who reclines at the table or the one who serves? Is it not the one who reclines at the table? But I am among you as the one who serves.

"You are the ones who have stood by Me in My trials; and just as My Father has granted Me a kingdom, I grant you that you may eat and drink at My table in My kingdom, and you will sit on thrones judging the twelve tribes of Israel."

Jesus Demonstrates Greatness

John 13:2-17

And during supper, the devil having already put into the heart of Judas Iscariot, the son of Simon, to betray Him, Jesus, knowing that the Father had handed all things over to Him, and that He had come forth from God and was going back to God, got up from supper and laid His outer garments aside; and He took a towel and tied it around Himself.

Then He poured water into the basin, and began washing the disciples' feet and wiping them with the towel which He had tied around Himself. So He came to Simon Peter. He said to Him, "Lord, You are washing my feet?"

Jesus answered and said to him, "What I am doing, you do not realize right now, but you will understand later."

Peter said to Him, "Never shall You wash my feet!"

Jesus answered him, "If I do not wash you, you have no place with Me."

Simon Peter said to Him, "Lord, then wash not only my feet, but also my hands and my head!"

Jesus said to him, "He who has bathed needs only to wash his feet; otherwise he is completely clean. And you are clean—but not all of you." For He knew the one who was betraying Him; it was for this reason that He said, "Not all of you are clean."

Then, when He had washed their feet, and taken His garments and reclined at the table again, He said to them, "Do you know what I have done for you? You call Me 'Teacher' and 'Lord'; and you are correct, for so I am. So if I, the Lord and the Teacher, washed your feet, you also ought to wash one another's feet. For I gave you an example, so that you also would do just as I did for you. Truly, truly I say to you, a slave is not greater than his master, nor is one who is sent greater than the one who sent him. If you know these things, you are blessed if you do them."

> *Jesus answered and said to him, "What I am doing, you do not realize right now, but you will understand later."*

Jesus Identifies His Betrayer

John 13:18–30

I am not speaking about all of you. I know the ones whom I have chosen; but this is happening so that the Scripture may be fulfilled, 'HE WHO EATS MY BREAD HAS LIFTED UP HIS HEEL AGAINST ME.' From now on I am telling you before it happens, so that when it does happen, you may believe that I am He. Truly, truly I say to you, the one who receives anyone I send, receives Me; and the one who receives Me receives Him who sent Me."

When Jesus had said these things, He became troubled in spirit, and testified and said, "Truly, truly I say to you that one of you will betray Me." The disciples began looking at one another, at a loss to know of which one He was speaking.

Lying back on Jesus' chest was one of His disciples, whom Jesus loved. So Simon Peter nodded to this disciple and said to him, "Tell us who it is of whom He is speaking."

He then simply leaned back on Jesus' chest and said to Him, "Lord, who is it?"

Jesus then answered, "That man is the one for whom I shall dip the piece of bread and give it to him." So when He had dipped the piece of bread, He took and gave it to Judas, the son of Simon Iscariot. After this, Satan then entered him. Therefore Jesus said to him, "What you are doing, do it quickly." Now none of those reclining at the table knew for what purpose He had said this to him. For some were assuming, since Judas kept the money box, that Jesus was saying to him, "Buy the things we need for the feast"; or else, that he was to give something to the poor.

So after receiving the piece of bread, he left immediately; and it was night.

Jesus Predicts Peter's Denial

Matthew 26:31–33; Luke 22:31–32; Matthew 26:34–35

Then Jesus said to them, "You will all fall away because of Me this night, for it is written: 'I WILL STRIKE THE SHEPHERD, AND THE SHEEP OF THE FLOCK WILL BE SCATTERED.' But after I have been raised, I will go ahead of you to Galilee."

But Peter replied to Him, "Even if they all fall away because of You, I will never fall away!"

"Simon, Simon, behold, Satan has demanded to sift you men like wheat; but I have prayed for you, that your faith will not fail; and you, when you have turned back, strengthen your brothers."

Jesus said to him, "Truly I say to you that this very night, before a rooster crows, you will deny Me three times."

Peter said to Him, "Even if I have to die with You, I will not deny You!"

All the disciples said the same thing as well.

Jesus in Agony

Matthew 26:36–42; Luke 22:43–44; Matthew 26:43–46

Then Jesus came with them to a place called Gethsemane, and told His disciples, "Sit here while I go over there and pray." And He took Peter and the two sons of Zebedee with Him, and began to be grieved and distressed. Then He said to them, "My soul is deeply grieved, to the point of death; remain here and keep watch with Me."

And He went a little beyond them, and fell on His face and prayed, saying, "My Father, if it is possible, let this cup pass from Me; yet not as I will, but as You will."

And He came to the disciples and found them sleeping, and He said to Peter, "So, you men could not keep watch with Me for one hour? Keep watching and praying, so that you do not come into temptation; the spirit is willing, but the flesh is weak."

He went away again a second time and prayed, saying, "My Father, if this cup cannot pass away unless I drink from it, Your will be done."

[Now an angel from heaven appeared to Him, strengthening Him. And being in agony, He was praying very fervently; and His sweat became like drops of blood, falling down upon the ground].

Again He came and found them sleeping, for their eyes were heavy. And He left them again, and went away and prayed a third time, saying the same thing once more. Then He came to the disciples and said to them, "Are you still sleeping and resting? Behold, the hour is at hand and the Son of Man is being betrayed into the hands of sinners. Get up, let's go; behold, the one who is betraying Me is near!"

Jesus Is Betrayed and Arrested

Matthew 26:47-56; Mark 14:43-52; Luke 22:47-53; John 18:2-11

And while He was still speaking, behold, Judas, one of the twelve, came accompanied by a large crowd with swords and clubs, who came from the chief priests and elders of the people.

Now he who was betraying Him gave them a sign previously, saying, "Whomever I kiss, He is the one; arrest Him." And immediately Judas went up to Jesus and said, "Greetings, Rabbi!" and kissed Him.

But Jesus said to him, "Judas, are you betraying the Son of Man with a kiss?"

Then they came and laid hands on Jesus and arrested Him. And behold, one of those who were with Jesus reached and drew his sword, and struck the slave of the high priest and cut off his ear.

Then Jesus said to him, "Put your sword back into its place; for all those who take up the sword will perish by the sword. Or do you think that I cannot appeal to My Father, and He will at once put at My disposal more than twelve legions of angels? How then would the Scriptures be fulfilled, which say that it must happen this way?"

And He touched his ear and healed him.

At that time Jesus said to the crowds, "Have you come out with swords and clubs to arrest Me as you would against a man inciting a revolt? Every day I used to sit within the temple grounds teaching, and you did not arrest Me. But all this has taken place so that the Scriptures of the prophets will be fulfilled." Then all the disciples left Him and fled.

A young man was following Him, wearing nothing but a linen sheet over his naked body; and they seized him. But he pulled free of the linen sheet and escaped naked.

Devotional Thoughts for Thursday

So much has taken place today. What stands out for you? Was it that the Sovereign Lord of heaven took on the role of the absent servant, and bowing before His disciples, He washed their feet one by one? Or maybe it was Christ's agonizing cries to His Father in heaven to be freed from the looming experience of the cross? Please take some time to ponder these awesome thoughts—and there may be others that come to mind as you read today's happenings.

Be blessed as you read the following quote:

"Turning away, Jesus … again … fell prostrate, overcome by the horror of a great darkness. The humanity of the Son of God trembled in that trying hour. He prayed not now for His disciples that their faith might not fail, but for His own tempted, agonized soul. The awful moment had come—that moment which was to decide the destiny of the world. [Yes,] the fate of humanity trembled in the balance. Christ might even now refuse to drink the cup apportioned to guilty man. It was not yet too late. He might wipe the bloody sweat from His brow, and leave man to perish in his iniquity. He might say, Let the transgressor receive the penalty for his sin, and I will go back to My Father. Will the Son of God drink the bitter cup of humiliation and agony? Will the innocent [One] suffer the consequences of the curse of sin…? The words fall tremblingly from the pale lips of Jesus, "O My Father, if this cup may not pass away from me, except I drink it, Thy will be done."

Having made the decision, He fell dying to the ground from which He had partially risen. Where now were His disciples, to place their hands tenderly beneath the head of their fainting Master, and bathe that brow, marred indeed more the sons of men? The Saviour trod the wine press alone, and of [all] the people there was none with Him." (Ellen G. White, The Desire of Ages, pp. 690–691)

FRIDAY

Jesus before the High Priest

John 18:12–14, 19–24

So the Roman cohort, the commander, and the officers of the Jews arrested Jesus and bound Him, and brought Him to Annas first; for he was the father-in-law of Caiaphas, who was high priest that year. Now Caiaphas was the one who had advised the Jews that it was in their best interest for one man to die in behalf of the people.

The high priest then questioned Jesus about His disciples, and about His teaching. Jesus answered him, "I have spoken openly to the world; I always taught in synagogues and in the temple area, where all the Jews congregate; and I said nothing in secret. Why are you asking Me? Ask those who have heard what I spoke to them. Look: these people know what I said."

But when He said this, one of the officers, who was standing nearby, struck Jesus, saying, "Is that the way You answer the high priest?"

Jesus answered him, "If I have spoken wrongly, testify of the wrong; but if rightly, why do you strike Me?"

So Annas sent Him bound to Caiaphas the high priest.

Jesus before the Sanhedrin

Matthew 26:57–66; Luke 22:63–65

Those who had arrested Jesus led Him away to Caiaphas, the high priest, where the scribes and the elders were gathered together. But Peter was following Him at a distance, as far as the courtyard of the high priest, and he came inside and sat down with the officers to see the outcome.

Now the chief priests and the entire Council kept trying to obtain false testimony against Jesus, so that they might put Him to death. They did not find any, even though many false witnesses came forward. But later on two came forward, and said, "This man stated, 'I am able to destroy the temple of God and to rebuild it in three days.'"

The high priest stood up and said to Him, "Do You offer no answer for what these men are testifying against You?" But Jesus kept silent. And the high priest said to Him, "I place You under oath by the living God, to tell us whether You are the Christ, the Son of God."

Jesus said to him, "You have said it yourself. But I tell you, from now on you will see the Son of Man sitting at the right hand of power, and coming on the clouds of heaven."

Then the high priest tore his robes and said, "He has blasphemed! What further need do we have of witnesses? See, you have now heard the blasphemy; what do you think?"

They answered, "He deserves death!"

The men who were holding Jesus in custody began mocking Him and beating Him, and they blindfolded Him and repeatedly asked Him, saying, "Prophesy, who is the one who hit You?" And they were saying many other things against Him, blaspheming.

Peter Denies Jesus and Weeps

Matthew 26:69–74; Luke 22:61–62

Now Peter was sitting outside in the courtyard, and a slave woman came to him and said, "You too were with Jesus the Galilean."

But he denied it before them all, saying, "I do not know what you are talking about."

When he had gone out to the gateway, another slave woman saw him and said to those who were there, "This man was with Jesus of Nazareth."

And again he denied it, with an oath: "I do not know the man."

A little later the bystanders came up and said to Peter, "You really are one of them as well, since even the way you talk gives you away."

Then he began to curse and swear, "I do not know the man!" And immediately a rooster crowed.

And then the Lord turned and looked at Peter. And Peter remembered the word of the Lord, how He had told him, "Before a rooster crows today, you will deny Me three times." And he went out and wept bitterly.

Jesus before Pilate

John 18:28–38

Then they brought Jesus from Caiaphas into the Praetorium, and it was early; and they themselves did not enter the Praetorium, so that they would not be defiled, but might eat the Passover. Therefore Pilate came out to them and said, "What accusation are you bringing against this Man?"

They answered and said to him, "If this Man were not a criminal, we would not have handed Him over to you."

So Pilate said to them, "Take Him yourselves, and judge Him according to your law."

The Jews said to him, "We are not permitted to put anyone to death." This happened so that the word of Jesus which He said, indicating what kind of death He was going to die, would be fulfilled.

Therefore Pilate entered the Praetorium again, and summoned Jesus and said to Him, "You are the King of the Jews?"

Jesus answered, "Are you saying this on your own, or did others tell you about Me?"

Pilate answered, "I am not a Jew, am I? Your own nation and the chief priests handed You over to me; what have You done?"

Jesus answered, "My kingdom is not of this world. If My kingdom were of this world, My servants would be fighting so that I would not be handed over to the Jews; but as it is, My kingdom is not of this realm."

Therefore Pilate said to Him, "So You are a king?"

Jesus answered, "You say correctly that I am a king. For this purpose I have been born, and for this I have come into the world: to testify to the truth. Everyone who is of the truth listens to My voice."

Pilate said to Him, "What is truth?"

And after saying this, he came out again to the Jews and said to them, "I find no grounds at all for charges in His case."

Judas Hangs Himself

Matthew 27:3-10

Then when Judas, who had betrayed Him, saw that He had been condemned, he felt remorse and returned the thirty pieces of silver to the chief priests and elders, saying, "I have sinned by betraying innocent blood."

But they said, "What is that to us? You shall see to it yourself!"

And he threw the pieces of silver into the temple sanctuary and left; and he went away and hanged himself.

The chief priests took the pieces of silver and said, "It is not lawful to put them in the temple treasury, since it is money paid for blood." And they conferred together and with the money bought the Potter's Field as a burial place for strangers. For this reason that field has been called the Field of Blood to this day.

Then that which was spoken through Jeremiah the prophet was fulfilled: "AND THEY TOOK THE THIRTY PIECES OF SILVER, THE PRICE OF THE ONE WHOSE PRICE HAD BEEN SET BY THE SONS OF ISRAEL; AND THEY GAVE THEM FOR THE POTTER'S FIELD, JUST AS THE LORD DIRECTED ME."

Jesus before Herod

Luke 23:4-12

But Pilate said to the chief priests and the crowds, "I find no grounds for charges in the case of this man."

But they kept on insisting, saying, "He is stirring up the people, teaching all over Judea, starting from Galilee, as far as this place!"

Now when Pilate heard this, he asked whether the man was a Galilean. And when he learned that He belonged to Herod's jurisdiction, he sent Him to Herod, since he also was in Jerusalem at this time.

Now Herod was overjoyed when he saw Jesus; for he had wanted to see Him for a long time, because he had been hearing about Him and was hoping to see some sign performed by Him. And he questioned Him at some length; but He offered him no answer at all. Now the chief priests and the scribes stood there, vehemently charging Him. And Herod, together with his soldiers, treated Him with contempt and mocked Him, dressing Him in a brightly shining robe, and sent Him back to Pilate. And so Herod and Pilate became friends with one another that very day; for previously, they had been enemies toward each other.

Jesus or Barabbas

Matthew 27:15–21; Luke 23:18–19; Matthew 27:22–31

Now at the Passover Feast the governor was accustomed to release for the people any one prisoner whom they wanted. And at that time they were holding a notorious prisoner called Barabbas. So when the people gathered together, Pilate said to them, "Whom do you want me to release for you: Barabbas, or Jesus who is called Christ?" For he knew that it was because of envy that they had handed Him over.

And while he was sitting on the judgment seat, his wife sent him a message, saying, "See that you have nothing to do with that righteous Man; for last night I suffered greatly in a dream because of Him."

But the chief priests and the elders persuaded the crowds to ask for Barabbas, and to put Jesus to death. And the governor said to them, "Which of the two do you want me to release for you?"

And they said, "Barabbas."

But they cried out all together, saying, "Away with this man, and release to us Barabbas!" (He was one who had been thrown into prison for a revolt that took place in the city, and for murder.)

Pilate said to them, "Then what shall I do with Jesus who is called Christ?"

They all said, "Crucify Him!"

But he said, "Why, what evil has He done?"

Yet they kept shouting all the more, saying, "Crucify Him!"

Now when Pilate saw that he was accomplishing nothing, but rather that a riot was starting, he took water and washed his hands in front of the crowd, saying, "I am innocent of this Man's blood; you yourselves shall see."

And all the people replied, "His blood shall be on us and on our children!"

Then he released Barabbas for them; but after having Jesus flogged, he handed Him over to be crucified.

Then the soldiers of the governor took Jesus into the Praetorium and gathered the whole Roman cohort to Him. And they stripped Him and put a red cloak on Him. And after twisting together a crown of thorns, they put it on His head, and put a reed in His right hand; and they knelt down before Him and mocked Him, saying, "Hail, King of the Jews!" And they spit on Him, and took the reed and beat Him on the head. And after they had mocked Him, they took the cloak off Him and put His own garments back on Him, and led Him away to crucify Him.

Jesus Crucified

Matthew 27:32-44; Mark 15:21-32; Luke 23:26-43; John 19:17-27

And they compelled a passer-by coming from the country, Simon of Cyrene (the father of Alexander and Rufus), to carry His cross.

Now following Him was a large crowd of the people, and of women who were mourning and grieving for Him. But Jesus turned to them and said, "Daughters of Jerusalem, stop weeping for Me, but weep for yourselves and for your children. For behold, days are coming when they will say, 'Blessed are those who cannot bear, and the wombs that have not given birth, and the breasts that have not nursed.' Then they will begin TO SAY TO THE MOUNTAINS, 'FALL ON US,' AND TO THE HILLS, 'COVER US.' For if they do these things when the tree is green, what will happen when it is dry?"

Now two others, who were criminals, were also being led away to be put to death with Him.

Then they brought Him to the place Golgotha, which is translated, Place of a Skull. And they tried to give Him wine mixed with myrrh; but He did not take it.

There they crucified Him and the criminals, one on the right and the other on the left.

[But Jesus was saying, "Father, forgive them; for they do not know what they are doing."]

Now it was the third hour when they crucified Him.

And those passing by were speaking abusively to Him, shaking their heads, and saying, "You who are going to destroy the temple and rebuild it in three days, save Yourself! If You are the Son of God, come down from the cross."

In the same way the chief priests also, along with the scribes and elders, were mocking Him and saying, "He saved others; He cannot save Himself! He is the King of Israel; let Him now come down from the cross, and we will believe in Him. HE HAS TRUSTED IN GOD; LET GOD RESCUE HIM NOW, IF HE TAKES PLEASURE IN HIM; for He said, 'I am the Son of God.'"

And the rebels who had been crucified with Him were also insulting Him in the same way.

One of the criminals who were hanged there was hurling abuse at Him, saying, "Are You not the Christ? Save Yourself and us!"

But the other responded, and rebuking him, said, "Do you not even fear God, since you are under the same sentence of condemnation? And we indeed are suffering justly, for we are receiving what we deserve for our crimes; but this man has done nothing wrong." And he was saying, "Jesus, remember me when You come into Your kingdom!"

And He said to him, "Truly I say to you, today you will be with Me in Paradise."

Now Pilate also wrote an inscription and put it on the cross. It was written: "JESUS THE NAZARENE, THE KING OF THE JEWS."

Therefore many of the Jews read this inscription, because the place where Jesus was crucified was near the city; and it was written in Hebrew, Latin, and in Greek. So the chief priests of the Jews were saying to Pilate, "Do not write, 'The King of the Jews'; rather, write that He said, 'I am King of the Jews.'"

Pilate answered, "What I have written, I have written."

Then the soldiers, when they had crucified Jesus, took His outer garments and made four parts: a part to each soldier, and the tunic also; but the tunic was seamless, woven in one piece. So they said to one another, "Let's not tear it, but cast lots for it, to decide whose it shall be." This happened so that the Scripture would be fulfilled: "THEY DIVIDED MY GARMENTS AMONG THEMSELVES, AND THEY CAST LOTS FOR MY CLOTHING." Therefore the soldiers did these things.

Now beside the cross of Jesus stood His mother, His mother's sister, Mary the wife of Clopas, and Mary Magdalene. So when Jesus saw His mother, and the disciple whom He loved standing nearby, He said to His mother, "Woman, behold, your son!" Then He said to the disciple, "Behold, your mother!" And from that hour the disciple took her into his own household.

Jesus Dies on the Cross

Matthew 27:45-56; Mark 15:33-41; Luke 23:44-49; John 19:28-30

When the sixth hour came, darkness fell over the whole land until the ninth hour. At the ninth hour Jesus cried out with a loud voice, "ELOI, ELOI, LEMA SABAKTANEI?" WHICH IS TRANSLATED, "MY GOD, MY GOD, WHY HAVE YOU FORSAKEN ME?"

And when some of the bystanders heard Him, they began saying, "Look! He is calling for Elijah!" And someone ran and filled a sponge with sour wine, put it on a reed, and gave Him a drink, saying, "Let us see if Elijah comes to take Him down."

After this, Jesus, knowing that all things had already been accomplished, in order that the Scripture would be fulfilled, said, "I am thirsty." A jar full of sour wine was standing there; so they put a sponge full of the sour wine on a branch of hyssop and brought it up to His mouth. Therefore when Jesus had received the sour wine, He said, "It is finished!" And He bowed His head and gave up His spirit.

And behold, the veil of the temple was torn in two from top to bottom; and the earth shook and the rocks were split. Also the tombs were opened, and many bodies of the saints who had fallen asleep were raised; and coming out of the tombs after His resurrection, they entered the holy city and appeared to many.

Now as for the centurion and those who were with him keeping guard over Jesus, when they saw the earthquake and the other things that were happening, they became extremely frightened and said, "Truly this was the Son of God!"

And all the crowds who came together for this spectacle, after watching what had happened, began to return home, beating their chests.

Now there were also some women watching from a distance, among whom were Mary Magdalene, Mary the mother of James the Less and Joses, and Salome. When He was in Galilee, they used to follow Him and serve Him; and there were many other women who came up with Him to Jerusalem.

Jesus' Side Is Pierced

John 19:31–37

Now then, since it was the day of preparation, to prevent the bodies from remaining on the cross on the Sabbath (for that Sabbath was a high day), the Jews requested of Pilate that their legs be broken, and the bodies be taken away. So the soldiers came and broke the legs of the first man, and of the other who was crucified with Him; but after they came to Jesus, when they saw that He was already dead, they did not break His legs. Yet one of the soldiers pierced His side with a spear, and immediately blood and water came out. And he who has seen has testified, and his testimony is true; and he knows that he is telling the truth, so that you also may believe. For these things took place so that the Scripture would be fulfilled: "NOT A BONE OF HIM SHALL BE BROKEN." And again another Scripture says, "THEY WILL LOOK AT HIM WHOM THEY PIERCED."

Jesus Buried in Joseph's Tomb

Mark 15:42–45; John 19:39, 41; Mark 15:46; John 19:42; Mark 15:47; Luke 23:55–56

When evening had already come, since it was the preparation day, that is, the day before the Sabbath, Joseph of Arimathea came, a prominent member of the Council, who was himself also waiting for the kingdom of God; and he gathered up courage and went in before Pilate, and asked for the body of Jesus. Now Pilate wondered if He was dead by this time, and summoning the centurion, he questioned him as to whether He was already dead. And after learning this from the centurion, he granted the body to Joseph.

Nicodemus, who had first come to Him by night, also came, bringing a mixture of myrrh and aloes, about a hundred litras weight.

Now in the place where He was crucified there was a garden, and in the garden was a new tomb in which no one had yet been laid.

Joseph bought a linen cloth, took Him down, wrapped Him in the linen cloth, and laid Him in a tomb which had been cut out in the rock; and he rolled a stone against the entrance of the tomb.

Therefore because of the Jewish day of preparation, since the tomb was nearby, they laid Jesus there.

Mary Magdalene and Mary the mother of Joses were watching to see where He was laid.

Now the women who had come with Him from Galilee followed, and they saw the tomb and how His body was laid. And then they returned and prepared spices and perfumes.

And on the Sabbath they rested according to the commandment.

Devotional Thoughts for Friday

The four Gospels present a detailed account of what happened to Jesus on this day: Jesus had had no food that morning to strengthen Him. What He did have, though, was the strength the angel brought Him from heaven the night before. His trial was illegal in that the Sanhedrin met during nighttime hours—something they never did. Our Savior stood on trial before them, the High Priest, Pilate, and Herod. Finally, He was brought to the governor where the people shouted that He should be crucified and the notorious Barabbas released.

> *The hours dragged by until finally Jesus cried out with a loud voice, "It is finished," and He breathed His last. The price for mankind's redemption had been paid. What does this day mean to you?*

Along the way He was mocked, beaten, spat upon, and a crown of thorns thrust upon His head. On top of all this, He watched as His most ardent follower, Peter, denied Him three times.

Then came the walk up the hill to the cross. There He was subjected to the agony of nails being pounded into His hands and feet and the extreme pain as the cross was lifted up and dropped into the ground. The hours dragged by until finally Jesus cried out with a loud voice, "It is finished," and He breathed His last. The price for mankind's redemption had been paid.

What does this day mean to you?

Consider this quote from *The Desire of Ages*:

The spotless Son of God hung upon the cross, His flesh lacerated with stripes; those hands so often reached out in blessing, nailed to the wooden bars; those feet so tireless on ministries of love, spiked to the tree; that royal head pierced by the crown of thorns; those quivering lips shaped to the cry of woe. And all that He endured—the blood drops that flowed from His head, His hands, His feet, the agony that racked His frame, and the unutterable anguish that filled His soul at the hiding of His Father's face—speaks to each child of humanity, declaring, It is for thee that the Son of God consents to bear this burden of guilt; for thee He spoils the domain of death, and opens the gates of Paradise. He who stilled the angry waves and walked the foam-capped billows, who made devils tremble and disease flee, who opened blind eyes and called forth the dead to life,—offers Himself upon the cross as a sacrifice, and this from love to thee. (White, *The Desire of Ages,* p. 755)

SABBATH

A Guard Is Set

Matthew 27:62-66

Now on the next day, that is, the day which is after the preparation, the chief priests and the Pharisees gathered together with Pilate, and they said, "Sir, we remember that when that deceiver was still alive, He said, 'After three days I am rising.' Therefore, give orders for the tomb to be made secure until the third day; otherwise, His disciples may come and steal Him, and say to the people, 'He has risen from the dead,' and the last deception will be worse than the first."

Pilate said to them, "You have a guard; go, make it as secure as you know how." And they went and made the tomb secure with the guard, sealing the stone.

Devotional Thoughts for Sabbath

What welcome peace and quietness for our Savior as He rested in the tomb. It is worth noting that Jesus didn't return to heaven when He died, so He couldn't promise the thief on the cross that he would be with Him that day.

Jesus, when He had arisen from the tomb the next morning, told Mary Magdalene not to touch Him for He had not gone to His Father in heaven yet.

As Jesus rested in the tomb on the Sabbath day, He was unaware of the many soldiers who were ordered by Pilate, at the priests' and elders' request, to guard the tomb. Every precaution was taken so that His disciples wouldn't be able to take Him away.

> As Jesus rested in the tomb on the Sabbath day, He was unaware of the many soldiers who were ordered by Pilate, at the priests' and elders' request, to guard the tomb. Every precaution was taken so that His disciples wouldn't be able to take Him away.

Yes, dear reader, Jesus' work was done. His mission accomplished. He wants us to rest from our labors on the Sabbath day and remember what He has done for us.

Consider this quote:

> *Weak men counseled and planned. Little did these murderers realize the uselessness of their efforts. But by their action God was glorified. The very efforts made to prevent Christ's resurrection are the most convincing arguments in its proof. The greater the number of soldiers placed around the tomb, the stronger would be the testimony that He had risen. Hundreds of years before the death of Christ, the Holy Spirit had declared through the psalmist, "Why do the heathen rage, and the people imagine a vain thing? The kings of the earth set themselves, and the rulers take counsel together, against the Lord, and against His anointed.... He that sitteth in the heavens shall laugh: the Lord shall have them in derision." Psalm 2:1–4. Roman guards and Roman arms were powerless to confine the Lord of life within the tomb. The hour of His release was near.* (White, *The Desire of Ages*, p. 778)

SUNDAY

He Is Risen

Mark 16:1, 3; Matthew 28:2-4; John 20:1-10

When the Sabbath was over, Mary Magdalene, Mary the mother of James, and Salome bought spices so that they might come and anoint Him.

They were saying to one another, "Who will roll away the stone from the entrance of the tomb for us?"

And behold, a severe earthquake had occurred, for an angel of the Lord descended from heaven and came and rolled away the stone, and sat upon it. And his appearance was like lightning, and his clothing as white as snow. The guards shook from fear of him and became like dead men.

Now on the first day of the week Mary Magdalene came early to the tomb, while it was still dark, and saw the stone already removed from the tomb. So she ran and came to Simon Peter and to the other disciple whom Jesus loved, and said to them, "They have taken the Lord from the tomb, and we do not know where they have put Him." So Peter and the other disciple left, and they were going to the tomb. The two were running together; and the other disciple ran ahead, faster than Peter, and came to the tomb first; and he stooped to look in, and saw the linen wrappings lying there; however he did not go in. So Simon Peter also came, following him, and he entered the tomb; and he looked at the linen wrappings lying there, and the face-cloth which had been on His head, not lying with the linen wrappings but folded up in a place by itself. So the other disciple who had first come to the tomb also entered then, and he saw and believed. For they did not yet understand the Scripture, that He must rise from the dead. So the disciples went away again to their own homes.

Mary Magdalene Sees Jesus

John 20:11–18

But Mary was standing outside the tomb, weeping; so as she wept, she stooped to look into the tomb; and she saw two angels in white sitting, one at the head and one at the feet, where the body of Jesus had been lying. And they said to her, "Woman, why are you weeping?"

She said to them, "Because they have taken away my Lord, and I do not know where they put Him." When she had said this, she turned around and saw Jesus standing there, and yet she did not know that it was Jesus.

Jesus said to her, "Woman, why are you weeping? Whom are you seeking?"

Thinking that He was the gardener, she said to Him, "Sir, if you have carried Him away, tell me where you put Him, and I will take Him away."

Jesus said to her, "Mary!"

She turned and said to Him in Hebrew, "Rabboni!" (which means, Teacher).

Jesus said to her, "Stop clinging to Me, for I have not yet ascended to the Father; but go to My brothers and say to them, 'I am ascending to My Father and your Father, and My God and your God.'"

Mary Magdalene came and announced to the disciples, "I have seen the Lord," and that He had said these things to her.

The Soldiers Are Bribed

Matthew 28:11–15

Some of the men from the guard came into the city and reported to the chief priests all that had happened. And when they had assembled with the elders and consulted together, they gave a large sum of money to the soldiers, and said, "You are to say, 'His disciples came at night and stole

Him while we were asleep.' And if this comes to the governor's ears, we will appease him and keep you out of trouble." And they took the money and did as they had been instructed; and this story was widely spread among the Jews and is to this day.

The Road to Emmaus

Luke 24:13–35

And behold, on that very day two of them were going to a village named Emmaus, which was sixty stadia from Jerusalem. And they were talking with each other about all these things which had taken place. While they were talking and discussing, Jesus Himself approached and began traveling with them. But their eyes were kept from recognizing Him.

And He said to them, "What are these words that you are exchanging with one another as you are walking?" And they came to a stop, looking sad. One of them, named Cleopas, answered and said to Him, "Are You possibly the only one living near Jerusalem who does not know about the things that happened here in these days?"

And He said to them, "What sort of things?"

And they said to Him, "Those about Jesus the Nazarene, who proved to be a prophet mighty in deed and word in the sight of God and all the people, and how the chief priests and our rulers handed Him over to be sentenced to death, and crucified Him. But we were hoping that it was He who was going to redeem Israel. Indeed, besides all this, it is now the third day since these things happened. But also some women among us left us bewildered. When they were at the tomb early in the morning, and did not find His body, they came, saying that they had also seen a vision of angels who said that He was alive. And so some of those who were with us went to the tomb, and found it just exactly as the women also had said; but Him they did not see."

And then He said to them, "You foolish men and slow of heart to believe in all that the prophets have spoken! Was it not necessary for the Christ to suffer these things and to come into His glory?" Then beginning with Moses and with all the Prophets, He explained to them the things written about Himself in all the Scriptures.

And they approached the village where they were going, and He gave the impression that He was going farther. And so they strongly urged Him, saying, "Stay with us, for it is getting toward evening, and the day is now nearly over." So He went in to stay with them.

And it came about, when He had reclined at the table with them, that He took the bread and blessed it, and He broke it and began giving it to them. And then their eyes were opened and they recognized Him; and He vanished from their sight.

They said to one another, "Were our hearts not burning within us when He was speaking to us on the road, while He was explaining the Scriptures to us?" And they got up that very hour and returned to Jerusalem, and found the eleven gathered together and those who were with them, saying, "The Lord has really risen and has appeared to Simon!" They began to relate their experiences on the road, and how He was recognized by them at the breaking of the bread.

Jesus Appears before His Disciples

Luke 24:36–43; John 20:19–23

Now when it was evening on that day, the first day of the week, and when the doors were shut where the disciples were together due to fear of the Jews, Jesus came and stood in their midst, and said to them, "Peace be to you."

But they were startled and frightened, and thought that they were looking at a spirit. And He said to them, "Why are you frightened, and why are doubts arising in your hearts? See My hands and My feet, that it is I Myself; touch Me and see, because a spirit does not have flesh and bones as you plainly see that I have."

And when He had said this, He showed them His hands and His feet. While they still could not believe it because of their joy and astonishment, He said to them, "Have you anything here to eat?" They served Him a piece of broiled fish; and He took it and ate it in front of them.

So Jesus said to them again, "Peace be to you; just as the Father has sent Me, I also send you." And when He had said this, He breathed on them and said to them, "Receive the Holy Spirit. If you forgive the sins of any, their sins have been forgiven them; if you retain the sins of any, they have been retained."

Devotional Thoughts for Sunday

The day which began with deep unbelief ended up filled with wonderful hope. Jesus told the women at the tomb to go and tell the disciples that He was alive. But would the disciples believe them? They were buried in sorrow that their Messiah had died and all their hopes of greatness with Him had perished.

> *How would you have liked to have been Mary Magdalene asking Jesus, whom she thought was the gardener, if He knew where the body of Jesus had been taken? Then to hear the voice of Jesus calling her name?*

Have you too had cherished hopes that died? How would you have liked to have been Mary Magdalene asking Jesus, whom she thought was the gardener, if He knew where the body of Jesus had been taken? Then to hear the voice of Jesus calling her name? This woman out of whom Jesus had cast seven devils was the first to see Him alive. What love and restoration there is for all us sinners!

Would you have liked to have been one of the two disciples who were on their way home after the crucifixion? What an experience it must have been to have had the Scriptures explained to them by the One who inspired the writing of them! Later that evening, as Jesus sat down to eat with them, they discovered that their companion was none other than Jesus Himself! Today we have the promise that the Holy Spirit will guide us as we ask Him to enlighten our minds as we read God's Word. Do we take as much advantage of this as we should?

Be blessed as you ponder the following quotation:

> *How many are still doing what those disciples did! How many echo Mary's despairing cry, "They have taken away the Lord, ... and we know not where they have laid Him"! To how many might the Savior's words be spoken, "Why weepest thou? whom seeketh thou?" He is close beside them, but their tear-blinded eyes do not discern Him. He speaks to them, but they do not understand. Oh that the bowed head might be lifted, that the eyes might be open to behold Him, that the ears might listen to His voice! "Go quickly, and tell His disciples that He is risen." Bid them look not to Joseph's new tomb, that was closed with a great stone, and sealed with the Roman seal. Christ is not there. Look not to the empty sepulcher. Mourn not as those who are hopeless and helpless. Jesus lives, and because He lives, we shall live also. From grateful hearts, from lips touched with holy fire, let the glad song ring out, Christ is risen! He lives to make intercession for us. Grasp this hope, and it will hold the soul like a sure, tried anchor. Believe, and thou shalt see the glory of God.* (White, *The Desire of Ages*, p. 794)

THE FORTY DAYS

Jesus Commissions His Disciples

Matthew 28:16–20; Mark 16:15–18

But the eleven disciples proceeded to Galilee, to the mountain which Jesus had designated to them. And when they saw Him, they worshiped Him; but some were doubtful. And Jesus came up and spoke to them, saying, "All authority in heaven and on earth has been given to Me. Go, therefore, and make disciples of all the nations, baptizing them in the name of the Father and the Son and the Holy Spirit, teaching them to follow all that I commanded you; and behold, I am with you always, to the end of the age."

And He said to them, "Go into all the world and preach the gospel to all creation. The one who has believed and has been baptized will be saved; but the one who has not believed will be condemned. These signs will accompany those who have believed: in My name they will cast out demons, they will speak with new tongues; they will pick up serpents, and if they drink any deadly poison, it will not harm them; they will lay hands on the sick, and they will recover."

Seeing and Believing
John 20:24–29

But Thomas, one of the twelve, who was called Didymus, was not with them when Jesus came. So the other disciples were saying to him, "We have seen the Lord!"

But he said to them, "Unless I see in His hands the imprint of the nails, and put my finger into the place of the nails, and put my hand into His side, I will not believe."

Eight days later His disciples were again inside, and Thomas was with them. Jesus came, the doors having been shut, and stood in their midst and said, "Peace be to you." Then He said to Thomas, "Place your finger here, and see My hands; and take your hand and put it into My side; and do not continue in disbelief, but be a believer."

Thomas answered and said to Him, "My Lord and my God!"

Jesus said to him, "Because you have seen Me, have you now believed? Blessed are they who did not see, and yet believed."

Breakfast by the Sea
John 21:1–14

After these things Jesus revealed Himself again to the disciples at the Sea of Tiberias, and He revealed Himself in this way: Simon Peter, Thomas who was called Didymus, Nathanael of Cana in Galilee, the sons of Zebedee, and two others of His disciples were together. Simon Peter said to them, "I am going fishing." They said to him, "We are also coming with you." They went out and got into the boat; and that night they caught nothing.

But when the day was now breaking, Jesus stood on the beach; yet the disciples did not know that it was Jesus. So Jesus said to them, "Children, you do not have any fish to eat, do you?"

They answered Him, "No."

And He said to them, "Cast the net on the right-hand side of the boat, and you will find the fish." So they cast it, and then they were not able to haul it in because of the great quantity of fish.

Therefore that disciple whom Jesus loved said to Peter, "It is the Lord!" So when Simon Peter heard that it was the Lord, he put on his outer garment (for he was stripped for work), and threw himself into the sea. But the other disciples came in the little boat, for they were not far from the land, but about two hundred cubits away, dragging the net full of fish.

So when they got out on the land, they saw a charcoal fire already made and fish placed on it, and bread. Jesus said to them, "Bring some of the fish which you have now caught."

So Simon Peter went up and hauled the net to land, full of large fish, 153; and although there were so many, the net was not torn.

Jesus said to them, "Come and have breakfast." None of the disciples ventured to inquire of Him, "Who are You?" knowing that it was the Lord. Jesus came and took the bread and gave it to them, and the fish likewise.

This was now the third time that Jesus revealed Himself to the disciples, after He was raised from the dead.

Peter Is Restored

John 21:15–19

Now when they had finished breakfast, Jesus said to Simon Peter, "Simon, son of John, do you love Me more than these?"

He said to Him, "Yes, Lord; You know that I love You." He said to him, "Tend My lambs."

He said to him again, a second time, "Simon, son of John, do you love Me?"

He said to Him, "Yes, Lord; You know that I love You." He said to him, "Shepherd My sheep."

He said to him the third time, "Simon, son of John, do you love Me?"

Peter was hurt because He said to him the third time, "Do you love Me?" And he said to Him, "Lord, You know all things; You know that I love You."

Jesus said to him, "Tend My sheep. Truly, truly I tell you, when you were younger, you used to put on your belt and walk wherever you wanted; but when you grow old, you will stretch out your hands and someone else will put your belt on you, and bring you where you do not want to go." Now He said this, indicating by what kind of death he would glorify God. And when He had said this, He said to him, "Follow Me!"

The Beloved Disciple

John 21:20–25

Peter turned around and saw the disciple whom Jesus loved following them—the one who also had leaned back on His chest at the supper and said, "Lord, who is the one who is betraying You?" So Peter, upon seeing him, said to Jesus, "Lord, and what about this man?"

Jesus said to him, "If I want him to remain until I come, what is that to you? You follow Me!"

Therefore this account went out among the brothers, that that disciple would not die; yet Jesus did not say to him that he would not die, but only, "If I want him to remain until I come, what is that to you?"

This is the disciple who is testifying about these things and wrote these things, and we know that his testimony is true.

But there are also many other things which Jesus did, which, if they were written in detail, I expect that even the world itself would not contain the books that would be written.

Jesus Ascends to Heaven

Mark 16:19–20; Luke 24:50–53; Acts 1:9–11

And He led them out as far as Bethany, and He lifted up His hands and blessed them.

And after He had said these things, He was lifted up while they were watching, and a cloud took Him up, out of their sight. And as they were gazing intently into the sky while He was going, then behold, two men in white clothing stood beside them, and they said, "Men of Galilee, why do you stand looking into the sky? This Jesus, who has been taken up from you into heaven, will come in the same way as you have watched Him go into heaven."

And they, after worshiping Him, returned to Jerusalem with great joy, and were continually in the temple praising God.

And they went out and preached everywhere, while the Lord worked with them, and confirmed the word by the signs that followed.

Concluding Devotional Thoughts

The "forty day story" begins with Jesus meeting with His disciples on the mountain He had appointed for them. He assures them that all authority had been given Him in heaven and on earth. Now He asks them to go into all the world and preach the gospel to all people. Isn't it true even today, Jesus asks us who believe on Him to go out and be witnesses for Him?

Two beautiful stories of disciple restoration follow. The first is about Thomas. He hadn't been present when Jesus had appeared to the disciples. He declared he wouldn't believe unless he could put his finger in the imprint of the nails in Jesus' hands and put his hand into His side. What a demand to restore belief! Have we experienced times when we found it hard to believe? We aren't alone. The next time when the disciples were together and Thomas was with them, Jesus tells Thomas to come feel His hands and side. He has no harsh words for him, only love. And so it is with us. Jesus is there to lovingly restore our faith if we will let Him.

> *Now He asks them to go into all the world and preach the gospel to all people. Isn't it true even today, Jesus asks us who believe on Him to go out and be witnesses for Him?*

The second story is about Peter, the ardent, overzealous Peter. Yes, he had promised that he would never abandon his Master, and then when his feet were put to the fire, as the expression goes, he forcefully denied his Lord three times. What a failure! But Jesus knew Peter's heart. As the disciples ate the breakfast which He had prepared by the sea, Jesus restored Peter before them all. What a wonderful story which brought transformation into Peter's life and made him the ardent worker for Christ we read about in the book of Acts. How about you and me? Have we at times misrepresented our Savior? If we have, He is always willing to forgive and heal if we ask Him.

We close with the wonderful account of Jesus ascending back to heaven. His work on earth was done. The disciples as they watched were told by two men dressed in white apparel, "Men of Galilee, why do you stand looking into the sky? This Jesus, who has been taken up from you into heaven, will come in the same way as you have watched Him go into heaven" (Acts 1:11).

Today we await that soon return of Jesus. What does this mean to you? We trust this book has, through the workings of the Holy Spirit, drawn you into a closer walk with the One who laid down His life for us.

Here is the final quote. Be blessed as you read it:

Christ had ascended to heaven in the form of humanity. The disciples had beheld the cloud receive Him. The same Jesus who had walked and talked and prayed with them; who had broken bread with them; who had been with them in their boats on the lake; and who had that very day toiled with them up the ascent of Olivet,—the same Jesus had now gone to share His Father's throne. And the angels had assured them that the very One whom they had seen go up into heaven, would come again even as He had ascended.... "The Lord Himself shall descend from heaven with a shout, with the voice of the Archangel, and with the trump of God: and the dead in Christ shall rise." "The Son of Man shall come in His glory, and all the holy angels with Him, then shall He sit upon the throne of His glory." ... 1 Thessalonians 4:16; Matthew 25:31. Thus will be fulfilled the Lord's own promise to His disciples: "If I go and prepare a place for you, I will come again, and receive you unto Myself; that where I am, there ye may be also." John 14:3. Well might the disciples rejoice in the hope of their Lord's return. (White, *The Desire of Ages*, pp. 831–832)

POSTSCRIPT

Reason to Believe

John 20:30–31

So then, many other signs Jesus also performed in the presence of the disciples, which are not written in this book; but these have been written so that you may believe that Jesus is the Christ, the Son of God; and that by believing you may have life in His name.

APPENDIX

Matthew was once a tax collector, and hence was well acquainted with lists and details. When he wrote to his fellow Jews, it was with the purpose of proving that Jesus was indeed the Messiah and also to explain to them the nature of God's kingdom.

Mark, however, was not one of the disciples. After he accompanied Paul on his first missionary journey, he wrote to encourage the Roman Christians, proving to them that—beyond a doubt—Jesus is our Messiah. By means of a rapid succession of vivid accounts, he describes Jesus in action. Jesus, he claims, is identified not so much by what He said, but by what He did.

Luke, a Greek, was a doctor, a gentile Christian, and a close friend of Paul. A man of detail, he begins his story by explaining his extensive research about Jesus. He has come to the conclusion that although Jesus was the divine Son of God, He was also the Son of Man.

John was the youngest of the disciples and the brother of James—also a disciple of Jesus. At first Jesus called them the "Sons of Thunder." However, Scripture tells us of the amazing transformation that Jesus wrought in John's life, to the point where he became known as the disciple of love. John wrote his Gospel to Christians and non-Christians after the destruction of Jerusalem in AD 70 and before his exile to the island of Patmos. Ninety percent of John's narrative is unique to him. His Gospel is not so much a description of the life of Christ but a powerful argument for the fact of his incarnation, a conclusive demonstration that Jesus was, and is, the very heaven-sent Son of God and the only source of eternal life.

The first three Gospels of the New Testament—Matthew, Mark, and Luke—have been called the synoptic Gospels because they look at the facts through the same eye. They give similar accounts of the ministry of Jesus; often with different and more or less detail but mostly following the same sequence and often using the same words.

The Gospel of John omits much of the material found in the synoptic Gospels and contains material that is not found in them. In the areas where

John does tell of the same events, he tends to add information that is not in the other Gospels.

This work does not attempt to be an exhaustive compilation of every parallel reference in the gospel story. It is a selection designed to convey a personal message. A good place to find a complete side-by-side presentation of the four Gospels is gospelparallels.com, "The Synoptic Gospel Parallels with John's Gospel," pages 1 and 2.

Following is a listing of the sections, or stories, contained in this book. For each section are references where it may be found in each Gospel. The references that are used in this book are highlighted in **bold**.

THURSDAY

Preparation for the Passover

Matthew 26:17–20; **Mark 14:12–16**; *Luke 22:7–14*

Mark and Luke give almost exactly the same account, while Matthew's is briefer. It is not found in John.

Jesus Remakes the Passover Supper

Matthew 26:26–29; Mark 14:22–25; **Luke 22:14–23**

Luke's account is the most detailed and the other two are almost identical. It is not found in John, which is odd since this supper becomes a centerpiece of Christianity. Instead, John simply states "And supper being ended." After describing the foot washing and identification of His betrayer, John has a long passage of Jesus giving His last words of comfort and advice to His disciples and finally a prayer.

The Disciples Argue about Greatness

Luke 22:24–30

Only Luke records the argument the disciples had during the Passover supper. But another similar argument occurred before Jesus entered Jerusalem the final time, when there was contention between the disciples as to who should be the greatest (Mark 10:41–45).

Jesus Demonstrates Greatness

John 13:2-17

This story of the foot washing is not found in the other Gospels. It is a touching demonstration of Jesus' admonition that "whosoever would be first among you, shall be servant of all" (mentioned by Mark and Luke).

Jesus Identifies His Betrayer

Matthew 26:21-25, 30; Mark 14:18-21, 26; Luke 22:21-23; **John 13:18-30**

John's account is the most detailed, describing the conversation between Peter and John, and then Jesus' urging to Judas to complete his task quickly. (See Mark 14:3-11 for Judas' initial contact with the priests to deliver Jesus to them.) Now he receives the money for the betrayal. Jesus quotes Psalm 41:9: "Even my close friend in whom I trusted, who ate my bread, has lifted up his heel against me."

Jesus Predicts Peter's Denial

Matthew 26:31-35; Mark 14:27-31; **Luke 22:31-32***; John 13:36-38*

Jesus quotes Zechariah 13:7, "Strike the Shepherd and the sheep will be scattered." He is foretelling the effect that His death will have on His followers.

Jesus in Agony

Matthew 26:36-46; Mark 14:32-42; **Luke 22:39-46**

The account of Jesus' prayer in the Garden of Gethsemane is interestingly not mentioned by John, though he does say the garden was a place that Jesus and His disciples frequented. Though Luke's account is the briefest, it is the most dramatic, describing the angel that came to strengthen Jesus and the sweat of His agony that was like great drops of blood. While Matthew and Mark describe the disciples' sleepiness as a weakness, Luke says they were "sleeping from sorrow."

Jesus Betrayed and Arrested

Matthew 26:47-56; Mark 14:43-52; Luke 22:47-53; John 18:2-11

John portrays Jesus as knowing what was about to happen. He says that Jesus came out to meet the rabble, asking whom they sought. While all four Gospels give an account of the servant's ear being cut off, only John identifies by name who wielded the sword and who lost his ear, and only Luke mentions that Jesus restored the ear. Only Mark mentions the young man who escaped capture by fleeing naked. It is thought that this young man was later the author of the Gospel according to Mark.

FRIDAY

Jesus before the High Priest

Matthew 26:57; Mark 14:53; Luke 22:54; **John 18:12–14, 19–24**

The Gospels are not clear as to the exact order of events here. John gives a detailed account of Jesus' questioning before Annas (the father of the high priest Caiaphas), but the other Gospels mention an appearance before the high priest and then the council, or Sanhedrin. Luke states that "When it was day, the Council of elders of the people assembled, both chief priests and scribes" (Luke 22:66).

Jesus before the Sanhedrin

Matthew 26:57–68; *Mark 14:53–65;* **Luke 22:63–71**; *John 18:12–14*

The Great Sanhedrin was the supreme council of the Jews in Jerusalem, which was the final authority on decisions that affected the religious and political life of all Jews. It had the power of life and death until Judea became subject to the Roman Empire. In New Testament times, it retained the power of passing sentences, but the Roman Empire decided whether to accept or reject verdicts and to carry out penalties.

Caiaphas, the high priest, had advised the Sanhedrin that it was "in their best interest for one man to die in behalf of the people" (John 18:14). Those who might have scruples about killing Jesus should think about the larger picture. His death would prevent Roman retribution and upheaval of national identity should Jesus proclaim Himself King.

Grief and mourning traditionally has been expressed among Jews by the tearing of one's clothes. But the high priest was forbidden by Levitical law to tear his clothes: "The priest who is highest among his brothers, on whose head the anointing oil has been poured and who has been consecrated to wear the garments, shall not uncover his head nor tear his clothes" (Lev. 21:10).

Peter Denies Jesus and Weeps

Matthew 26:69-75; Mark 14:66-72; **Luke 22:54-62***; John 18:15-18, 25-27*

John's account is rather brief and lacking the vehement outbursts of denial followed by bitter remorse of the other Gospels.

Jesus before Pilate

Matthew 27:1-2, 11-14; Mark 15:1-5; Luke 23:1-5; **John 18:28-38, 19:1-4**

Unlike the other Gospels in which Jesus hardly speaks, John details the conversation between Pilate and Jesus, in which Pilate tries to understand the nature of Jesus' claim to kingship.

Judas Hangs Himself

Matthew 27:3-10

This tragic end of Jesus' betrayer is recorded by only one Gospel. The quotation recorded in Matthew, "AND THEY TOOK THE THIRTY PIECES OF SILVER …" (v. 9) is thought to refer to Zechariah 11:12-13 or possibly Jeremiah 18:1-11 and Jeremiah 32:6-9. However, careful reading suggests that neither is likely. It is possible that the reference is to a passage that has been lost.

Jesus before Herod

Luke 23:4-12

Only Luke records the appearance before Herod.

Jesus or Barabbas

Matthew 27:15-40; Mark 15:6-19; **Luke 23:13-25***; John 18:39-40, 19:1-19*

Matthew and Mark give the most detail about this story. Interestingly, John emphasizes Jesus' conversation with Pilate and barely mentions Barabbas.

Jesus Crucified

Matthew 27:32-44; Mark 15:21-32; Luke 23:26-43; **John 19:17-27**

John differs from the other Gospels by stating Jesus bore His own cross. The others give the burden to Simon of Cyrene. It is Luke who records the many women who followed Jesus' procession to Golgotha and His prediction of worse calamities to come.

Mark 15:28, "And the scripture was fulfilled, which saith, And he was numbered with the transgressors" (KJV), is not included in the 2020 edition of NASB as it is not present in the earliest manuscripts. It is a quotation from Isaiah 53:12: "Therefore, I will allot Him a portion with the great, and He will divide the plunder with the strong, because He poured out His life unto death, and was counted with wrongdoers; yet He Himself bore the sin of many, and interceded for the wrongdoers." Three times Jesus shared the lot of the transgressors, by His birth of a woman, baptism by John, and finally dying as a criminal.

When speaking to the women who followed Him, Jesus quoted Hosea 10:8, "They will say to the mountains, 'Cover us!' And to the hills, 'Fall on us!'"

Luke 23:43 states, "And He said to him, 'Truly, I say to you, today you will be with Me in Paradise.'" This implies that Jesus and the man crucified with Him went to paradise that day. But how could that be, since Jesus would not rise from the dead until the third day? This conundrum can be resolved by either interpreting Jesus to be speaking figuratively or that the punctuation is misplaced. By simply moving the comma, the meaning is changed: "Assuredly, I say to you today, you will be with Me in Paradise."

John quotes Psalm 22:18, "They divide my garments among them, and they cast lots for my clothing."

Jesus Dies on the Cross

Matthew 27:45–56; Mark 15:33–41; Luke 23:44–49; John 19:28–30

Jesus quotes Psalm 22:1: "My God, my God, why have You forsaken me? Far from my help are the words of my groaning."

Just before He died, Jesus said "I thirst!" Perhaps this was a quotation from Psalm 69:21. He was offered sour wine on a sponge. This most likely was "posca," a drink that was popular with the Roman soldiers. It was a mixture of wine vinegar and water and considered a good thirst quencher.

Crucifixion was a long, agonizing death. It caused death not from the hand and leg wounds but by suffocation. To breathe, it was necessary to push up from the legs to relieve constriction placed on the chest caused by hanging from the hands. Death came slowly as fatigue and pain made it harder to breathe. To hasten death, the legs were broken, making it very hard to breathe (See William D. Edwards, Wesley J. Gabel, and Floyd E. Hosmer, "On the Physical Death of Jesus Christ," *JAMA* 255, no. 11 (March 21, 1986)).

Jesus' Side Is Pierced

John 19:31–37

Only John records the piercing of Jesus' side by a spear. It would have, without doubt, killed Him if He was not already dead. No one could claim that Jesus was not really dead when He was taken down from the cross.

"NOT A BONE OF HIM SHALL BE BROKEN" (John 19:36) is a quotation from Psalm 34:20, and "THEY WILL LOOK AT HIM WHOM THEY PIERCED" (v. 7) is from Zechariah 12:10.

Jesus Buried in Joseph's Tomb

Matthew 27:57–61; **Mark 15:42–47;** *Luke 23:50–56; John 19:38–42*

Joseph of Arimathea was from the Judean town of Arimathea. He was a member of the Sanhedrin who opposed the council's verdict. Nicodemus was a Pharisee who had previously visited Jesus at night. Both were secret followers of Jesus, but at His death, they showed courage to ask Pilate for Jesus' body. By the time He was removed from the cross, it was very late in the day. So He was hastily placed in a nearby tomb and the usual burial rites were postponed until after the Sabbath.

SABBATH

A Guard Is Set

Matthew 27:62–66

This day has only one recorded event and is told by only one Gospel.

SUNDAY

He Is Risen

Matthew 28:1–10; **Mark 16:1–11;** *Luke 24:1–11;* **John 20:1–10**

Each Gospel has a slightly different story to share. It is worthwhile to read each one. The women are told to tell the disciples of Jesus' resurrection. Peter is mentioned separately because of his denial of Jesus.

The disciples did not recall Psalm 16:10: "For You will not abandon my soul to Sheol; you will not allow Your Holy One to undergo decay."

Mary Magdalene Sees Jesus

Mark 16:9; ***John 20:11–18***

This detailed account of Jesus appearing to Mary Magdalene is told only by John.

The Soldiers Are Bribed

Matthew 28:11–15

Only Matthew records the chief priests buying the soldier's silence.

The Road to Emmaus

Mark 16:12–13; ***Luke 24:13–35***

While Mark and Luke record this story, Mark mentions it only briefly. The distance from Jerusalem to Emmaus was about seven miles or eleven kilometers. The two disciples did not recognize Jesus until He broke bread at the evening meal. In the Gospels, Jesus is frequently portrayed as breaking bread before a meal. He must have done it in such a way that was unique to Him. His disciples identified that action as being a key part of their identity, especially in the Lord's Supper.

Jesus Appears before His Disciples

Luke 24:36–43; John 20:19–23

At a time when the disciples were still in the depths of despair, not daring to believe that Jesus really had risen from the dead, Jesus appeared to an assembly of them. The disciples naturally thought that a ghost had appeared and were terrified. Jesus sought to prove His corporeal existence by asking for food and eating it before them.

THE FORTY DAYS

The forty days refers to the time from the resurrection until the ascension of Jesus. Most of the events during the forty days are recounted by John.

Jesus Commissions His Disciples

Matthew 28:16–20; Mark 16:15–18

Seeing and Believing

John 20:24–29

The disciple Thomas has been called the "doubter" because he refused to believe that Jesus had risen. Jesus met those doubts by showing Thomas evidence of His crucifixion and then gently reproved him by saying "Blessed are they who did not see, and yet believed" (verse 29).

Breakfast By the Sea

John 21:1–14

This story illustrates Jesus' continued interest in His disciples' welfare.

Peter Is Restored

John 21:15–19

This story cements Peter's standing among the disciples after having denied Jesus and is told only by John. It is interesting that in John's account, Peter plays a prominent role and is mentioned frequently along with John.

The Beloved Disciple

John 21:20–25

When referring to himself, John never uses his own name. Instead he is "the one whom Jesus loved."

Jesus Ascends to Heaven

Mark 16:19–20; Luke 24:50–53; Acts 1:9–11

Only two of the Gospels end with Jesus' ascension. A short paragraph is taken from the book of Acts. While it is not a Gospel, it is thought to have been written by Luke. The reader is encouraged to read all three accounts as they differ slightly.

Reason to Believe

John 20:30–31

We conclude with a quote from John's Gospel which summarizes the purpose of his Gospel and the reason for this book. We hope that your heart has been touched and your spirit uplifted.

RESOURCES

Devotionals
Pages 18, 28, 30, 35, 40

Artwork
Pages xii, 13, 19, 24, 30, 32, 37, 43

BIBLIOGRAPHY

Edwards, William D., Wesley J. Gabel, and Floyd E. Hosmer. "On the Physical Death of Jesus Christ." *JAMA* 255. No. 11. March 21, 1986.

"The Synoptic Gospel Parallels with John's Gospel." Gospel Parallels. *https://www.gospelparallels.com* (last modified August 31, 2023).

White, Ellen G. *The Desire of Ages*. Mountain View, CA: Pacific Press, 1898.

We invite you to view the complete
selection of titles we publish at:
www.TEACHServices.com

We encourage you to write us
with your thoughts about this,
or any other book we publish at:
info@TEACHServices.com

TEACH Services' titles may be purchased in
bulk quantities for educational, fund-raising,
business, or promotional use.
bulksales@TEACHServices.com

Finally, if you are interested in seeing
your own book in print, please contact us at:
publishing@TEACHServices.com
We are happy to review your manuscript at no charge.

www.ingramcontent.com/pod-product-compliance
Lightning Source LLC
Chambersburg PA
CBHW042137160426
43200CB00019B/2961